EXTINCT LAND MAMMALS

and those in danger of extinction

Philip Steele

Franklin Watts

London New York Sydney Toronto

© 1991 Zoe Books Limited

Devised and produced by
Zoe Books Limited
15 Worthy Lane
Winchester
Hampshire SO23 7AB
England

First published in 1991
in Great Britain by
Franklin Watts Ltd
96 Leonard Street
London EC2A 4RH

First published in Australia by
Franklin Watts Australia
14 Mars Road
Lane Cove
New South Wales 2066

ISBN 0 7496 0420 4

A CIP catalogue record for this book is
available from the British Library.

Printed in the United Kingdom

Consultant: Professor Richard T.J. Moody,
BSc, Dip Ed, PhD, FGS
Design: Julian Holland Publishing Ltd
Picture researcher: Jennifer Johnson
Illustrator: Cecilia Fitzsimons
Cartography: Gecko Ltd

Photograph acknowledgements
pp17 Roger Tidman/NHPA, 19 Jany
Sauvanet/NHPA, 21 Hans Reinhard/Bruce
Coleman Ltd, 22 Bruce Coleman Ltd, 23
GeoScience Features, 24 Jane Burton/
Bruce Coleman Ltd, 25 J L G Grande/
Bruce Coleman Ltd, 26 Erwin & Peggy
Bauer/Bruce Coleman Ltd, 27 Philippa
Scott/NHPA.

Contents

The Quagga

There was once an animal called the Quagga. It was a member of the horse family and a close relative of the zebra. Herds of quaggas used to live on the grasslands of South Africa alongside ostrich and wildebeeste. Their only enemy was the lion, that used to hunt the quaggas for food.

In the 19th century, white farmers took over the country of peoples such as the Hottentots. The farmers started to graze cattle on the land once grazed by the quaggas. The farmers had guns and lassos and hunted from horseback. The quaggas were easy prey, and were soon gunned down. Their hides were used to make sacks and bags. The meat was used as food. Between 1840 and 1878, the wild Quagga was destroyed forever. It became extinct.

Some of the quaggas had been captured and taken to zoos. However, they did not breed easily in captivity. The last quagga of all died in Amsterdam Zoo in the Netherlands on 12 August 1883.

▶ The quaggas were swift, tough animals with a good sense of hearing. A fully grown quagga stood nearly 1.5 m (5 ft) at the shoulder. It had reddish-brown stripes around its head, neck and shoulders, but its hind-quarters, legs and belly were unmarked. Its mane stood up in brown and white bands.

DID YOU KNOW?
- The Quagga's name came from a word used by the Hottentot people of South Africa, *quabkah*. They used it to describe the neighing sound made by zebras and quaggas.
- In the 1830s, quaggas were used to draw smart carriages through the streets of London, England.

1835-1837 Dutch farmers move northwards through South Africa. Shooting of quagga herds begins on a large scale.
1870 Last wild quagga killed.
1883 Last quagga dies in a zoo.

Fossils

Many mammals became extinct long before humans even existed. When these creatures died, their remains were often pressed into soft mud or tar. Over millions of years, the mud and tar turned to stone. The weight of new layers of mud or tar pressed down on them. The remains and marks left behind are called fossils. When fossils are discovered, they help scientists find out more about animals that lived on Earth thousands of years ago.

▼ The first mammals we know of were like shrews. Fossil remains of *Morganucodon* have been found in Wales and China. They show that *Morganucodon* was only 10 cm (4 in) from nose to tail, and had a thin body with grasping hands. It ate insects, and scientists think that it may have hunted at night because it had large eyes.

▶ *Borhyaena* ate small animals and had sharp teeth suitable for cracking open bones. *Borhyaena* was a marsupial. Like kangaroos and koalas today, *Borhyaena* kept its young in a pouch until they were big enough to look after themselves. Fossils of *Borhyaena* have been found in South America. They show that *Borhyaena* was 1 m (3 ft) from nose to tail.

MAMMALS
- The first mammals evolved from mammal-like reptiles called synapsids. Mammals are warm-blooded: they are able to control their own body heat.
- A mammal is a creature which gives birth to live young, which it feeds on its own milk.
- There are about 4230 different kinds, or species, of mammals in the world today. About 650 of these species are endangered.

215 million years ago: Age of mammals begins.
c200 million years ago: *Morganucodon* lives on Earth.
30 million years ago: *Borhyaena* lives on Earth.

A changing world

There are many reasons why animals become extinct. They are often hunted and killed by humans or other animals. Sometimes their food supply is destroyed by a sudden change in climate, or other animals take over their territory. Creatures that cannot cope with a changing world die out.

When animals do adapt, or change to meet new conditions, new kinds of animals may gradually develop. This process is called evolution.

Giant sloths

About 35 million years ago, giant ground sloths evolved in what is now South America. They were slow, shambling creatures which fed on leaves. The largest was *Megatherium* which was 6 m (20 ft) from nose to tail.

The ground sloths became extinct 11,000 years ago, but no-one knows why. It is possible that changes in the climate had an effect, but it is probable that early hunters killed many of them for food.

11,000 years ago: Giant sloth extinct. 10,000-13,000 years ago: *Diprotodon* extinct.

DID YOU KNOW?
- *Diprotodon* was the largest marsupial the world has ever known. It was 3 m (9 ft) from nose to tail.
- Australia separated from the other land masses about one hundred million years ago when the mammals that lived there were all marsupials. Apart from some bats and rodents, all the advanced, or placental mammals that live there were introduced by people.

Diprotodon

Wombats are Australian marsupials that can burrow in the soil. The largest ones alive today measure a little over 1 m (3 ft). In prehistoric times, however, giant wombats browsed among the bushes eating leaves.

Wombats like *Diprotodon* evolved about 12 million years ago, but they died out only several thousand years ago. Scientists think that Aboriginal people crossing from New Guinea to Australia hunted *Diprotodon* to extinction.

▼ *Diprotodon* had a large head with a skull which measured over 1 m (3 ft) in length. Its long front teeth were used to strip bushes of their leaves. *Diprotodon's* thick legs and clawed feet gave it a shambling walk.

Woolly Mammoths

About one and a half million years ago the climate of the world became much colder. This led to the caps of ice around the North and South Poles spreading to cover much of North America and Northern Europe. Such periods of cold climate are called ice ages.

The Woolly Mammoth lived in northern parts of the world between 300,000 and 10,000 years ago. It was a favourite prey of Stone Age hunters, who used its coat for clothes, and the meat as food.

A fully grown adult Woolly Mammoth measured 3 m (10 ft) to the shoulder and looked like an elephant with huge tusks. However, it had a hairy coat to keep it warm and a fatty hump to provide it with a good reserve of energy during harsh winters. When the ice ages ended and the climate became warmer, the Woolly Mammoth did not adapt to the new conditions. It became extinct.

▶ The Woolly Mammoth was well adapted to the cold conditions of its time, with its long furry coat and small ears. It was not much larger than today's elephants but its tusks were enormous. They could grow to 5 m (16 ft) in length.

DID YOU KNOW?
- The last ice sheets disappeared about 10,000 years ago.
- Complete mammoth carcasses have been found in the frozen ground of the Siberian tundra in the Soviet Union.

5 million years ago: Mammoth species evolve in Africa.
300,000 years ago: Mammoths spread through Europe, Asia and North America.
10,000 years ago: Mammoths become extinct as the climate changes.

Hunted to extinction

For thousands of years, humans had only simple weapons made of wood, stone and bone. Over the ages they developed better weapons which made hunting easier. In recent history people began to realize that animals were being hunted to the point of extinction.

The Aurochs

The Aurochs was a huge wild ox which once lived in most parts of Europe and Asia. Although it was very fierce and powerful, it had been trapped and hunted for so long that by the eleventh century, it was found only in the wilder parts of Eastern Europe. In 1299 a Polish duke passed a law which banned the hunting of Aurochs. However, over the years the numbers of Aurochs became smaller and smaller until the last one died in 1627.

1299 First ban on hunting Aurochs in Poland.
1599 Small herd of Aurochs left in west Poland.
1627 Last Aurochs dies near Warsaw.
1800 Blaauwbok extinct.
1876 Last Tarpan killed in the Ukraine.

▼ The Aurochs was 1.8 m (6 ft) high at the shoulder, and had a black hide. Spanish fighting bulls are probably still very close to the original Aurochs breed.

LOST TO THE HUNTERS

- The Blaauwbok, a goat-like antelope living in South Africa, was hunted to extinction by about 1800.
- The Eastern Elk, a type of deer, had become extinct in the USA by the early 1880s.
- The last wild Tarpan was shot in Russia in 1876.
- Seven sub-species of the Grey Wolf have become extinct this century.

▲ The grassy plains of Central Asia and Eastern Europe were once the home of a beautiful wild horse called the Tarpan. It was grey or fawn, with a black mane and tail, and stood 1.3 m (4.3 ft) high. When firearms were invented, Tarpan were hunted with guns.

The Thylacine

The British founded a settlement in Australia in 1788. During the following years, Europeans explored Australia, farming, mining and building cities. They hunted and killed many of the native marsupial animals, such as the kangaroos and opossums. Animals such as sheep, camels, foxes and rabbits were introduced into the country by the settlers. These new animals competed with the native animals for food and territory.

The Thylacine was sometimes known as the Tasmanian Wolf or Tiger. It was a strange creature, for although it looked like a stripy wolf, it was a marsupial. Its total length was 1.8 m (6 ft) and it had a tail similar to a kangaroo's. It lived on the island of Tasmania, off the south coast of Australia.

The white settlers hated the Thylacine, as they thought it killed their sheep. In fact, although it could be very fierce, the Thylacine ate birds, kangaroos and wallabies, and did little harm to the settlers' flocks of sheep.

▶ The Thylacine had a head like a wolf's. Its coat was fawn with dark stripes on its back. Like other marsupials, the Thylacine carried its young in a pouch.

RECENT SIGHTINGS?
- The Thylacine may not be extinct. Many people, including experienced trackers and wildlife experts, have sighted dog-like animals with stripy markings. These have been seen not only on Tasmania, but on the Australian mainland as well.
- A computer has been used to work out the most likely places for Thylacines to be found if they are not extinct. These places match exactly the location of the sightings.

1933 Thylacine possibly extinct in the wild.
1934 Last captive Thylacine dies in Hobart, Tasmania.

In danger

In recent years, the threat to land mammals has increased. One of the greatest dangers is the loss of their natural surroundings or habitat. In 1700 about 60 per cent of the planet was covered in forest. By the year 2000, only 25 per cent will be forested. The trees have been cut down to make way for towns and roads. Humans have also changed the environment, introducing new plants and animals to regions where they would not normally live. This often disturbs or destroys the native wildlife.

If a certain kind of plant disappears, the animal that feeds upon it may become extinct. In turn, this may affect larger animals that prey on the smaller ones. Changes to the food chain have happened naturally for millions of years on the planet. However, when prehistoric animals died out, there was the chance of new life forms evolving. Today, the natural world is less able to support a rich variety of wildlife because so much land is used by people.

DID YOU KNOW?
- Gorillas are the largest apes alive today. The tallest Mountain Gorilla on record measured over 1.8 m (6 ft).
- The Mountain Gorilla is hairier than its lowland cousins. It lives at heights of 2700 m (9000 ft).
- People used to think that gorillas were savage, dangerous creatures. Today we know that they are gentle giants that eat only plants.

IN NEED OF PROTECTION
- Many species of lemur live in the forests of Madagascar, a large island off the coast of Africa. As the forests have been cut down, the survival of the lemurs has been threatened. Although game reserves and parks have been created to protect them, 25 species of lemur are at risk. The largest endangered lemur is the Indris, 73 cm (29 in) long from nose to tail. It rarely survives in captivity.
- The Woolly Spider Monkey lives in the rain forests of Brazil. Destruction of its forest habitat has endangered this species which is now protected by laws. However, the monkey and many other threatened creatures will only be saved if the forest itself is protected.

The Mountain Gorilla

The Mountain Gorilla can be found only in about 20,000 sq km (7722 sq mi) of tropical African forest. There are very few gorillas left, and those are on the endangered species list prepared by the International Union for the Conservation of Nature and Natural Resources (IUCN). Changes in farming and herding methods have destroyed parts of the Gorilla's habitat, so it is protected in a number of national parks and reserves.

▼ The Mountain Gorilla is a massive ape. It weighs 200 kg (441 lb) and has a total length of 1.7 m (5.6 ft). It eats leaves, stems and shoots.

The Giant Panda

In 1869, a French priest called Père Armand David was exploring the remote mountain regions of south-west China. In the dense bamboo forests, his scouts discovered a strange mammal that looked like a cross between a bear and a raccoon. It weighed 180 kg (397 lb), measured up to 1.6 m (5 ft) in length, including its tail, and ate the shoots, stalks and leaves of bamboo plants. This rare creature was the Giant Panda, until then unknown to the outside world.

Today, the Giant Panda is found only in a small area of the Chinese provinces of Sichuan and Yunnan. It is difficult to track and keep watch on the panda, but it is thought that 600 or more may live in the wild today, and its numbers seem to be remaining steady.

The Giant Panda is not on the brink of extinction. However, it has to be protected because it is so rare. In the past, it has been hunted and some areas of its habitat have been cleared and settled by humans.

▶ The Giant Panda has a large head, and its thick fur is marked in black and white, with black patches around its eyes. It is a fussy eater, needing a plentiful supply of bamboo plants.

DID YOU KNOW?
● Breeding captive pandas is very difficult indeed. The Chinese have the best record. When a panda called Mei Mei gave birth to her sixth cub at Chengdu Zoo, the Chinese government awarded her a special medal!
● China has cooperated with the World Wide Fund for Nature in protecting pandas in the wild. There are now 12 reserves designated for the Giant Panda.

◀ The Giant Panda is used as the symbol of the World Wide Fund for Nature. It was chosen because of its popularity and appealing appearance.

Big cats

The tiger is the largest member of the cat family, weighing up to 230 kg (507 lb), and measuring 2.7 m (9 ft) from nose to tail. The first tigers lived in the cold forests of Siberia, in what is now the Soviet Union. Over thousands of years, different breeds evolved. Some lived in the forests of tropical Asia and adapted to life in a warm climate. Some lived in swamps and others lived in rocky mountain habitats.

As forests were cut down and swamps drained, these cats came into contact with humans more and more. Tigers were and are feared, although only a few of them are a danger to people. Thousands of tigers have been shot or poisoned because people feared they might be maneaters. All tigers are under threat and their survival is in the balance. During the 1970s the World Wide Fund for Nature set up reserves to protect the tiger in India and Nepal, as it is unlikely that it can survive without protection.

DID YOU KNOW?
- Only about 2500 Bengal Tigers survive today. There were more than 40,000 only 75 years ago.
- The Balinese Tiger is probably extinct. It has not been seen since 1952.
- In the last century and early years of this century, tiger hunting was a popular "sport" in India. Europeans and Indian princes, often riding on elephants, would shoot tigers with guns. Thousands of the big cats were slaughtered.

UNDER THREAT
- All 36 species of wild cat are threatened in one way or another. These include the Cheetah, the fastest mammal on land, the Florida Cougar and the Ocelot.
- One of the rarest big cats is the Snow Leopard of Central Asia. It has been hunted for its soft grey fur, and shot by herdsmen protecting their flocks.

▲ The Bengal Tiger has a golden coat, with white face markings and creamy belly fur. Its dark stripes provide camouflage as it moves through the shadowy undergrowth of the forest.

Tigers are protected in reserves but elsewhere they are still hunted. As the population of India and Bangladesh grows, there are fewer wild places where the tiger can thrive. Tigers need to hunt over a wide area to catch enough to eat.

The ivory trade

The African elephant is the largest land mammal living in the world today. It can measure up to 3 m (10 ft) at the shoulder and weighs 5 tonnes. While the elephant has done well in game reserves, its way across open countryside has been blocked by the building of towns and farms. Unable to move freely, elephant herds damage property and trample down fences.

The elephant has no natural enemies, but poachers kill it for its tusks. The tusks are sold to be carved into ornaments, chess pieces and jewellery. This trade, based in Hong Kong and Japan, is now strictly controlled, but illegal trading in ivory still continues.

THE ASIAN ELEPHANT
● The Asian elephant is smaller than its African cousin. It has smaller ears on its domed head, and shorter tusks. Females sometimes have no tusks at all.
● Fewer than 55,000 Asian elephants are thought to survive in the wild, and the forests where they live are being destroyed. They are also hunted for their tusks, about 50 being shot illegally each week in Burma alone.

◀ These game wardens have seized elephant tusks from poachers in Kenya.

DID YOU KNOW?

- Fewer than 2000 elephants survive in Kenya.
- The ivory trade results in the death of thousands of elephants each year. In the 1970s, the slaughter reached 100,000 a year. By the 1980s this figure had been reduced to about 30,000.
- The African elephant is listed by the IUCN as vulnerable. The Asian elephant is listed as endangered.
- Elephants are related to extinct prehistoric mammals such as the mammoths.

▼ Before widespread human settlement, African elephants wandered over huge distances. The trees they damaged in their search for the tender leaves on which they like to feed had time to grow again. Today, elephants are confined to smaller areas and can easily destroy their own habitat.

Small mammals

It is not only lumbering giants such as elephants that are at risk. Smaller mammals, including many rodents, find it hard to survive today. This is especially true on islands, where mammal species evolved and adapted to a particular climate or diet. If their food source is destroyed, the species cannot survive. For example, in the Caribbean islands, species of long-tongued bats, rice rats, spiny rats and muskrats have all become extinct due to loss of habitat or food source.

Many smaller mammals were destroyed when people introduced dogs, cats and other hunting animals to a remote area. The Kiore, or Polynesian Rat, was a plant-eating rodent which lived in New Zealand. It was killed by other species of rats which were brought to the islands on ships from Europe.

THREATENED SPECIES
The IUCN Red List of threatened small mammals includes:
- over 45 species of rodent
- 5 members of the rabbit family
- 19 members of the weasel and otter family
- 54 bat species.

▼ A Long-tailed Chinchilla in the Andes mountains, South America. Chinchillas used to be hunted for their soft grey fur as early as the 18th century. Fortunately, when they were threatened with extinction earlier this century, laws were passed which made it illegal to hunt these rodents in the wild. To prevent poaching, commercial farms have been set up which produce chinchilla fur for the traders. Today wild chinchillas are only found high in the Andes mountains and the Long-tailed Chinchilla is known to be severely at risk.

Homeless bats

Bats have many problems. The insects they eat have been killed by farmers and gardeners who use insecticides to protect plants. The attics where the bats roost are treated against woodworm. The chemicals used can poison bats. Caves and old mineshafts, once homes for many bats, have been filled in.

This has meant that, in the British Isles, numbers of the Greater Horseshoe Bat have dropped by more than 98 per cent over the last hundred years. Other more common bats have also become threatened. It has now been made illegal to disturb bats or to remove them from attic spaces.

▼ The Greater Horseshoe Bat grows up to 69 mm (2.75 in) in length, with a wingspan of up to 40 cm (15.75 in). It is found in southern and western Europe, as far north as Wales. It needs a safe place to hibernate in winter, where the temperature stays about 6°C (43°F). A safe haven is increasingly hard to find.

Wildlife survival

Land mammals are in danger all over the world, but many people are now working to save the world's wildlife. Scientists make detailed studies of animals and their behaviour. Game reserves and national parks offer animals a place to live where their habitat is protected and hunting is illegal. In 1975, an international treaty was drawn up to control trading in endangered species. Groups such as the World Wide Fund for Nature help to organize the protection of animals in the wild. The problems are immense. The interests of the wild animals often conflict with the needs of humans. However, some animals have been rescued from the verge of extinction and a few species are now being reintroduced into the wild after successful breeding programmes.

SAVED FROM EXTINCTION
● The Golden Lion Tamarin of Brazil is one endangered species that has been bred in captivity. Specimens from Jersey Zoo, in the Channel Islands, have been reintroduced to their native home, where they have bred in the wild.

◀ In the 1830s, the North American prairies were still grazed by herds of bison, or buffalo, up to a million strong. By 1890, only 9000 survived. They had been shot in their thousands by hunters such as "Buffalo Bill" Cody. In 1905, it was agreed that the North American bison should be saved from extinction. Bison were bred in captivity, and today they can be seen in reserves such as Yellowstone National Park in Wyoming.

Operation oryx

The Arabian Oryx is a beautiful long-horned antelope which lives in the deserts of the Middle East. Herds of oryx used to be chased and shot by hunters in jeeps. By the 1960s, the oryx was facing extinction. Wild oryx were captured and taken to the United States. Breeding programmes began at Phoenix and Los Angeles zoos, and in Saudi Arabia. By 1976, it was possible to release oryx that had been raised in captivity back into the Jordanian desert.

▼ The Arabian Oryx is only 1 m (39 in) high at the shoulder. Its magnificent horns are as long again. These were once prized by hunters as a trophy. The body of the oryx is white with brown legs and darker markings on its head. It was once widespread in the Arabian peninsula, Syria and Iraq.

Glossary

adapt To change or adjust to new living conditions.

camouflage The way in which the colour or shape of an animal disguises it against a natural background. This protects it against its enemies and helps it catch its prey.

endangered At risk of dying out.

evolution The development of new kinds of creatures or plants as they adapt to changed living conditions.

extinct No longer living. Scientists now declare a creature to be officially extinct when it has not been seen in the wild for 50 years.

fossil The remains of ancient animals or plants preserved in rock.

habitat The place that an animal makes its home.

ice age One of several periods in the Earth's history when the climate became much colder.

insecticides Chemicals that are used to kill insects.

mammal A warm-blooded animal which gives birth to live young which feed on the mother's milk. Mammals have four legs and are usually covered with fur.

marsupial A mammal which gives birth to young that are not fully developed. They cannot survive on their own. The young are kept in a pouch on the mother's body until they have grown bigger.

rodent A small mammal which has teeth for gnawing or nibbling.

species A single group of identical animals or plants that can breed to produce like offspring.

synapsids Prehistoric reptiles which developed hair and were probably warm-blooded. The first mammals evolved from such creatures.

vegetation The kind of plants found in any one region.

vulnerable Being few in number. These mammals are at risk of becoming endangered because of the threat to their habitat or because of hunting.

warm-blooded Having a body with a controlled temperature.

Find out more

- Many big cities have a Natural History or Science Museum, where you can see fossils of extinct creatures, and displays that show how they lived. The British Museum of Natural History in Cromwell Road, London SW7 5BD, is one of the best known of these museums.

- Are you interested in helping to protect endangered mammals around the world? The World Wide Fund for Nature has a junior membership. Contact Panda House, Weyside Park, Catteshall Lane, Godalming, Surrey GU7 1XR, for details of regional activities.

- There are zoos and wildlife parks in most regions of the British Isles. Do not go just to look – observe carefully how animals live and behave. Find out if the zoo has been working on any breeding projects with endangered species.

- Mammal-watching is not always as easy as bird-watching in the British Isles, but if you look closely you will see traces of wild mammals. Some, such as foxes, can now be seen at night even in cities. Hedgehogs, rodents and squirrels are often seen. Watch them closely and note their routes and feeding habits.

Time chart

PREHISTORIC PERIOD		
Years ago	**Human history**	**Natural history**
215 million		Mammals evolve from reptiles.
200 million		*Morganucodon* alive.
35 million		Giant sloths evolve.
30 million		*Borhyaena* alive.
12 million		Giant wombats evolve.
5 million		Early mammoths evolve.
4 million	"Ape-people", such as *Australopithecus,* evolve.	
100 000	Modern people evolve, hunters with weapons of stone.	

HISTORIC PERIOD		
10,000BC	Climatic change and possibly hunting by humans lead to extinction of many large mammals.	Woolly Mammoth extinct.
10,000-1500BC	Spread of farming. Taming of animals for food, wool and hide. Hunting and snaring of smaller mammals, as well as the surviving larger ones.	
1500BC-AD800	Classical period in Europe, followed by so-called Dark Ages. Clearance of forest, spread of human settlement.	Loss of habitat.
AD800–1450	Middle Ages in Europe, clearance of forest for farming. Europeans begin to explore rest of world.	Loss of habitat. Aurochs endangered.
1450-1700	Europeans colonise foreign lands, bringing firearms and introducing exotic animals.	Aurochs extinct (1627). 11 Caribbean rodents extinct.
1700-1800	European settlements spread in Americas. More efficient firearms for hunting. New farming methods. Beginnings of industry.	Blaauwbok hunted to extinction (by 1800). 2 Caribbean rodents extinct.
1800-1900	European settlements spread in Australia and New Zealand. Railways, large cities, factories and pollution. Rapid firearms and hunting on a vast scale. Massacre of bison in North America. Scientists learn about evolution and extinction.	5 Caribbean bats and 7 rodents extinct. 2 Australian marsupials extinct. Atlas Brown Bear extinct (1870s). Warrah (Falkland Islands Wolf) extinct (1876). Tarpan extinct (1876). Eastern Elk extinct (1880s). Quagga extinct (1883).
1900-	Motor transport, factories, pollution, deforestation, pesticides. Growth of conservation movements, such as International Union for Conservation of Nature and Natural Resources, and World Wide Fund for Nature. International treaties such as Convention on International Trade in Endangered Species.	Probable extinctions include 8 Australian marsupials, the Syrian Onager, a zebra sub-species, 2 reindeer, 2 antelope, 1 deer, sub-species of tiger and lion. Over 500 mammal species are now listed as endangered.

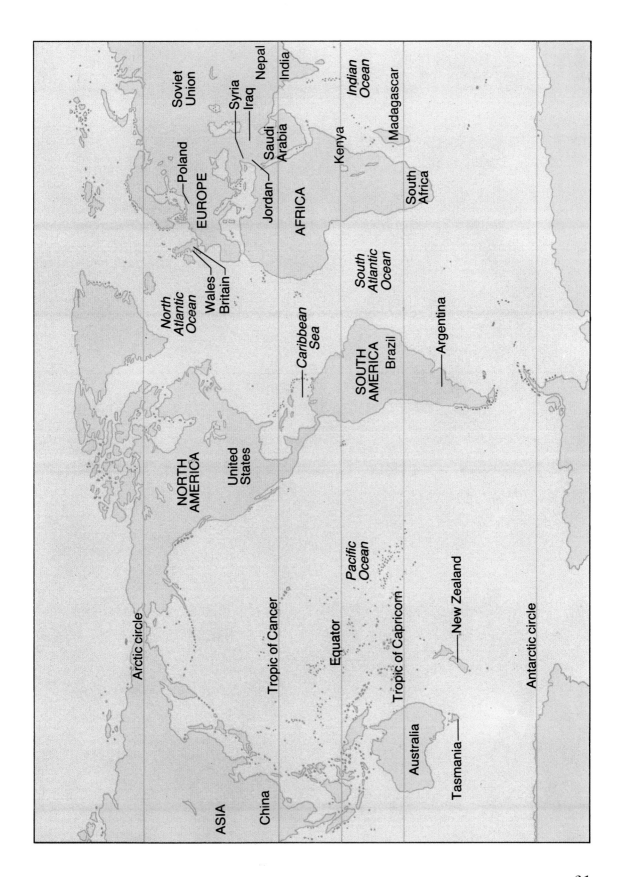

Index